KENNETH COPELAND

THE FORCE OF RIGHTEOUSNESS

KENNETH
COPELAND
PUBLICATIONS

Unless otherwise noted, all scripture is from the *King James Version* of the Bible.

Scripture quotations marked *New King James Version* are from the *New King James Version* © 1982 by Thomas Nelson, Inc.

Scipture quotations marked *The Amplified Bible* are from *The Amplified Bible, Old Testament* © 1965, 1987 by the Zondervan Corporation. *The Amplified New Testament* © 1958, 1987 by The Lockman Foundation. Used by permission.

The Force of Righteousness

ISBN-10 0-938458-12-4   30-0005
ISBN-13 978-0-938458-12-8

16 15 14 13 12 11   14 13 12 11 10 9

Kenneth Copeland Publications
Fort Worth, TX 76192-0001

For more information about Kenneth Copeland Ministries, call 800-600-7395
or visit www.kcm.org.

TABLE OF Contents

I believe the one thing holding more Christians in bondage than anything else is a lack of knowledge of righteousness. Unfortunately, over the years, we have developed some religious words and ideas that we place one meaning on at church and an entirely different meaning on in our daily lives. *Righteousness* is one of these words.

God's plan of redemption would be of no value to sinful men if it did not include righteousness and its mighty force. Righteousness is the key word to the revelation which the Apostle Paul received from Jesus.

As you read this book, I believe you will begin to understand why I get more excited preaching the righteousness of God and its force in the life of a believer than anything else.

Kenneth Copeland

chapterone
The Force of Righteousness

chapterone

The Force of Righteousness

Therefore if any man be in Christ, he is a new
creature: old things are passed away; behold, all
things are become new. And all things are of God,
who hath reconciled us to himself by Jesus Christ,
and hath given to us the ministry of reconciliation;
to wit, that God was in Christ, reconciling the
world unto himself, not imputing their trespasses
unto them; and hath committed unto us the word
of reconciliation. Now then we are ambassadors for
Christ, as though God did beseech you by us: we
pray you in Christ's stead, be ye reconciled to God.
For he hath made him to be sin for us, who knew
no sin; that we might be made the righteousness of
God in him (2 Corinthians 5:17-21).

Any person who is in Christ is a new creature, or a new creation. (The literal Greek says he is a new species of being which never existed before.) He has been completely re-created. Old things are passed away, all things are new, and all things are of God—not part God and part Satan. Some people think that a man is a schizophrenic when he becomes a Christian—that he has both the nature of God and the nature of Satan—but this is not so.

> *Any person who is in Christ is a new species of being which never existed before.*

In the new birth, a man's spirit is completely reborn; then it's his responsibility to renew his mind to the Word of God and use the Word to take control of his body.

Paul wrote to the believers in Rome, who were born-again, Spirit-filled Christians, and instructed them to renew their minds with the Word (Romans 12:2). Their faith was known throughout the world, but still they had not learned how to control their minds and bodies with the Word. He wrote to the church at Ephesus along the same lines saying, "You have put off the old man and put on the new man, so quit lying and cheating and acting ugly toward one another" (Ephesians 4:22-25). All these people were believers. They had been re-created—they had been made the righteousness of God—but most of them didn't know it!

Second Corinthians 5:21 tells us that God made Jesus, who knew no sin, to be sin for us "that we might be made the righteousness of God in him." As believers in Jesus Christ, we are the righteousness of God Himself!

What is righteousness? It is not a "goody-goody" way of acting or something that can be attained. Righteousness is a free gift of God, provided by Jesus at Calvary through the grace of God. Now, I'm not referring to our own righteousness—the Bible says that in the eyes of God "all our righteousness are as filthy rags" (Isaiah 64:6). However, we have been given the righteousness of God in Jesus Christ.

Through our traditional thinking, we have confused righteousness with holiness. We think righteousness is the way you act, but this is not true. Holiness is your conduct; righteousness is what you are—the nature of God.

Let me make this clearer. The word translated *righteousness* literally means "in right-standing." We have been put in right-standing with God.

> *Holiness is your conduct; righteousness is what you are, the nature of God.*

Jesus is the Mediator between God and man. When a man accepts Jesus, he is moved into a position of new birth. He enters into the kingdom of God as God's very own child and a joint heir with Jesus Christ. Consequently, there are certain privileges, rights and freedoms he has as a child of God because he is in right-standing with Him.

chaptertwo
Accepted in the Beloved

Accepted in the Beloved

We didn't get in right-standing with God by being good and acting right. We got there through faith in Jesus Christ and His redemptive work at Calvary. When we accepted the sacrifice of Jesus and made Him the Lord of our lives, then God accepted us. He had to! You see, God had already accepted Jesus' work on the cross. He judged it as good, glorified Jesus, and set Him at His own right hand in the heavenlies. He called Jesus "God" and inaugurated Him into the highest office in the whole universe. Therefore, the Father accepts us when we accept Jesus. Our conduct has absolutely nothing to do with it!

Let's look at 2 Corinthians 5:19. "To wit [or to know], that God was in Christ, reconciling the world unto himself, not imputing their trespasses unto them...." In other words, God does not hold our sins and trespasses against us. Very rarely has this whole gospel been preached—only pieces of it!

We have heard that God will not forgive a sinner until he confesses his sin, but this is not true. God has already provided forgiveness and is not holding our trespasses against us. This teaching about confession stems from 1 John 1:9. "If we confess our sins, he is faithful and just to forgive us...." However, this letter was written to Christians—to believers—to teach them how to maintain their fellowship with God.

The Apostle John wrote, "My little children, these things write I unto you, that ye sin not. And if any man sin, we have an advocate with the Father, Jesus Christ the righteous: And he is the propitiation for our sins: and not for ours only, but also for the sins of the whole world" (1 John 2:1-2).

John was referring to the sins of a Christian and instructing his fellow believers to partake of Jesus' advocate ministry. John 3:16 says, "For God so loved the world, that he gave his only begotten Son...." God loved us and Jesus gave Himself for us while we were in sin. God is not holding our trespasses against us. He is calling us to make Jesus our Lord. He accepted us on the basis of Jesus' right-standing with the Father and, in turn, made us in right-standing with Him. The only sin keeping anyone out of the kingdom of God is the sin of rejecting Jesus and what He has already provided (John 16:9).

As a citizen of the United States, you have certain rights, outlined in the Constitution, called "The Bill of Rights." (Actually, using Old English terminology, this would be called

"The Bill of Righteousness.") As long as you obey the laws of the land, you are in right-standing with the United States government.

The same thing is true with God. As a believer, you are a citizen of the kingdom of God and have a right to everything in the kingdom. There is a covenant between Jesus and God, signed in the blood of the Lamb— Jesus—which provides these rights

God accepted us on the basis of Jesus' right-standing with the Father, and in turn, made us in right-standing with Him.

for you. If Jesus is your Lord, then you are in right-standing with God—you have the righteousness of God (whether or not you partake of it). You have a right to everything God has. This is staggering to the human mind, but nevertheless, it's true. Jesus said, "Fear not, little flock; for it is your Father's good pleasure to give you the kingdom" (Luke 12:32).

chapterthree
Sin
Consciousness

chapterthree

Sin Consciousness

"For the law having a shadow of good things to come, and not the very image of the things, can never with those sacrifices which they offered year by year continually make the comers thereunto perfect" (Hebrews 10:1). Under Levitical Law, an animal had to be offered every 12 months to atone for the sins of the people. The word *atonement* means "to cover." This word is not found in the Greek New Testament when it refers to Jesus' sacrifice.

The word we translate *atonement* really means "to remit," or "to do away with." These Old Testament sacrifices could not completely do away with sin, they simply covered it for a year. However, the blood of Jesus didn't just cover sin, it remitted sin—it did away with it completely!

With these thoughts in mind, let's read verse 2: "For then would they [the sacrifices] not have ceased to be offered? Because that the worshippers once purged should have had no more conscience of sins." If the blood of calves and goats had cleansed them of sin, then they would have had no more conscience of sin, or a sin consciousness.

> *The blood of Jesus did not just cover sin, it did away with sin completely.*

Sin consciousness produces defeat and a false sense of humility. It attempts to be humble by defrauding itself and pushing itself back. But the Lord did not say, "Deface yourself." He said to think of others more highly than you think of yourself. This means that even when you are standing tall as the righteousness of God, you should elevate your fellow Christian above yourself, making both of you stand tall. When you deface yourself, you make yourself lower than you are.

If you were to ask most Christians, "Are you righteous?" they would say, "Me? No!" They are trying to be humble. They're afraid God wouldn't like it if they said they were righteous. Actually, they're speaking from the way they feel—from the way they've been trained—from ignorance of the Word of God concerning righteousness.

This type of sin consciousness has caused us to center on and preach sin, instead of righteousness. Actually, we have preached a form of condemnation on ourselves, but Romans 8:1 says, "There is therefore now no condemnation to them which are in Christ Jesus...." We have carried "sin tags" with us which are stumbling blocks in our growth as Christians.

Every time we start toward the righteousness of God, Satan jumps up in our paths and says, "Remember the ugly things you've done? Don't expect God to forget all that! Who do you think you are? You're too unworthy to approach God!" But the Word says the blood of Jesus purged our sins—they no longer exist. So we should take the Name of Jesus and drive out this sin consciousness.

What do I mean by a "sin tag"? A good example is, "Well, I'm just an old sinner saved by grace." No, you *were* an old sinner, but you got saved by grace! Now you are a born-again child of God!

Almost everyone is familiar with this scripture: "For all have sinned, and come short of the glory of God" (Romans 3:23). This scripture has been used untold numbers of times in preaching sin. But the Apostle Paul, in writing this letter to the body of believers in Rome, was instructing them about righteousness. Let's read this whole portion of Scripture:

When you elevate your fellow Christian above yourself, it makes both of you stand tall.

> But now the righteousness of God without the law is manifested, being witnessed by the law and the prophets; even the righteousness of God which is by faith of Jesus Christ unto all and upon all them that believe: for there is no difference: for all have sinned, and come short of the glory of God; being

justified freely by his grace through the redemption that is in Christ Jesus: whom God hath set forth to be a propitiation through faith in his blood, to declare his righteousness for the remission of sins that are past, through the forbearance of God; to declare, I say, at this time his righteousness: that he might be just, and the justifier of him which believeth in Jesus (Romans 3:21-26).

This is one sentence, constructed around the righteousness of God. Through sin consciousness, we have taken out one phrase—the only verse not referring to righteousness—and preached it with no mention of the other verses. Therefore, everyone knows about sin, but not many know about the righteousness of God. We are well aware of what we have been born out of, but have no idea what we have been born into! Colossians 1:12-13 says, "Giving thanks unto the Father...who hath delivered us from the power of darkness, and hath translated us into the kingdom of his dear Son."

chapterfour

Faith in Your Righteousness

chapterfour

Faith in Your Righteousness

You are a born-again child of the living God. It's time you began believing in the new birth and what Jesus has provided for you. You will realize that the Father has invited you to come boldly (confidently, without fear) to the throne of grace with your needs and requests. The Bible says when we pray according to His will, we know He hears us and we know that we have the petitions we desired of Him (1 John 5:14-15).

When we pray in the Name of Jesus, we immediately get the ear of God. First Peter 3:12 says, "For the eyes of the Lord are over the righteous, and his ears are open unto their prayers..." and James wrote that "the effectual fervent prayer of a righteous man availeth much" (James 5:16).

The following is an example of prayer from this righteousness consciousness:

Father, I see in Your Word that I have been made the righteousness of God in Christ Jesus. He has provided certain rights for me, and healing is one of these rights. I receive it now in Jesus' Name, and I thank You for it. Your Word also says that You are faithful and just to forgive me of my sins when I confess them, so I take this opportunity to confess this sin and get it out of my life, in order to maintain my complete fellowship with You. I receive Your forgiveness now in the Name of Jesus. I may not feel righteous—I may not feel forgiven—but Your Word says it, so it must be true. Satan, I now put on the breastplate of righteousness and come against you with the sword of the Spirit. Healing belongs to me. My body belongs to the God of this universe. I have given my body to Him, so in the Name of Jesus Christ of Nazareth, take your sickness and disease and get out!

A righteousness consciousness expects God's Word to be true and plans for success.

You have a *right* to expect your heavenly Father to answer. You have not prayed in your own name—you have prayed in Jesus' Name. His righteousness (right-standing with God) is yours! A righteousness consciousness expects God's Word to be true and plans for success.

This kind of prayer is tough in the world of the spirit, and it will bring results in the physical world. After you have prayed to God and taken authority over Satan, you should take authority over your physical body.

Speak to it in the Name of Jesus and command it to conform to the Word of God that says it is healed by the stripes of Jesus. I have done this and had my body shape up immediately.

> *When a person receives salvation, he is put into right-standing with God and re-created by the Spirit of God as if sin had never existed!*

You see, *the world of the spirit controls the world of the natural.*

A Spirit created all matter—His Name is Almighty God, and He is our Father! The righteousness of God is what it's all about!

Folks, it's time to believe the Word of God. Did you know that there is no longer a sin problem? Jesus solved it! He stopped the law of sin and death at the Cross and Resurrection. When a person receives salvation, he is put into right-standing with God and re-created by the Spirit of God as if sin had *never* existed! The only problem we have is the sinner problem. It's man's choice. All we need to do is choose righteousness and walk away from the sin problem.

It's time to move in line with this revelation. You *were* a sinner—you *have been* forgiven. You are now His workmanship, created in Christ Jesus! Begin to stand on this, instead of your past life. As far as God is concerned, your past life is forgotten. Now *you* need to forget it.

Your past life died the death of the Cross. In Galatians

2:20, the Apostle Paul said it this way: "I am crucified with Christ: nevertheless I live; yet not I, but Christ liveth in me...." As I was studying the Word one day, I noticed the Apostle Paul, in writing to the church at Corinth, said, "Receive us; we have wronged no man, we have corrupted no man, we have defrauded no man" (2 Corinthians 7:2). When I read this, it startled me, and I said, "Lord, I've caught the Apostle Paul in a lie! I know he wronged and defrauded men. He persecuted the Christians, putting them in prison for no legal reason. He stood by and watched as Stephen was stoned to death!" But the Spirit of God spoke to my heart strongly and said, *You watch who you call a liar! The man you are talking about died on the road to Damascus!*

You see, the Apostle Paul could write to the church at Corinth with a clear conscience and complete freedom of spirit saying, "We have wronged no man...we have defrauded no man." Paul realized the power of the gospel to raise him up when he was dead in trespasses and sins. He accepted the fact that he was a new creation in Christ Jesus—that his old spirit was dead and gone—that his past sins were forgiven and forgotten. Paul was born of God, and the power and force of righteousness was at work in his life.

chapterfive
Conformity With God

chapterfive

Conformity With God

We have discussed the fact that Jesus was aware of His rights—His righteousness—with God. He relied on it completely during His earthly ministry and ministered freely. He did what the Father told Him to do. This is the key to the mystery: The Father was in Jesus and Jesus was in the Father—*they were One*. Jesus' will conformed completely to the will of God. They walked together and worked together in total harmony. This is how believers are to live with God—not His will deforming ours nor our will bucking against His, but both wills conformed to each other.

Conformity with God is a much higher way of life than just merely being in submission to Him. When you conform to God, when you conform to His will and do His work, you'll reach a point where you'll lean entirely on your right-standing with Him. Then you, like Jesus, will not hesitate to lay hands on the sick and expect God to heal them. You will freely exercise your rights in the kingdom of God as His child and as a joint heir with Jesus.

When you lean entirely on your right-standing with Him, then you, like Jesus, will not hesitate to lay hands on the sick and expect God to heal them.

God sees you through the blood of the Lamb. He sees you the same as He sees Jesus. This is almost more than the human mind can conceive, but it's true! I'll prove it to you from the prayers of Jesus Himself. Jesus knew how to pray, and if anyone on earth could get his prayers answered, Jesus could. Therefore, it would be to our advantage to examine some of the things He prayed.

In John 17:20-21, Jesus is praying to God at a vital time in His earthly ministry. It is just moments before Calvary and He says, "Neither pray I for these alone [His disciples], but for them also which shall believe on me through their word" (verse 20). This includes you and me because each of us received Jesus, either directly or indirectly, through the words of one or more of these men.

So Jesus is referring to us and prays, "That they all may be one; *as thou, Father, art in me, and I in thee...*" (verse 21). Here is the example we are to follow in being one with each other, in conforming to one another and in conforming to Jesus. We are to be one with the Father as Jesus was One with Him. First Corinthians 6:17 says, "But he that is joined unto the Lord is one spirit." Another translation says, "He who is joined to the Lord is one spirit with Him" (New King James Version).

The Holy Spirit is the life force of God, and He lives in the heart of a believer. We get our life from Him. As Jesus taught in John 15:5, He is the vine and we are the branches. Praise the Lord!

When you begin to operate in these things, when you begin to act on the righteousness which Jesus has given you, you'll realize that many of the differences which have separated the Body of Christ for years are actually foolish and unimportant. We have bickered and fought with one another over the most ridiculous issues.

Jesus goes on in John 17:23 and prays to the Father to show them, "...that You have loved them [even] as You have loved Me" (The Amplified Bible). God loves you as much as He loves Jesus! He sees you as equal with Jesus—in His eyes, there is no difference. Begin to see

> God sees you as equal with Jesus—there is no difference in His eyes.

yourself as God sees you and take advantage of His free gift of righteousness. Your right-standing with God was bought with a high price...don't take it lightly. The Father's heart was hungry for a family, and Jesus freely gave Himself for this desire. What an act of love!

chaptersix

The Gift of
Righteousness

chaptersix

The Gift of Righteousness

For if by one man's offence death reigned by one;
much more they which receive abundance of
grace and of the gift of righteousness shall reign in
life by one, Jesus Christ.... For as by one man's
disobedience many were made sinners, so by the
obedience of one shall many be made righteous
(Romans 5:17, 19).

Here again, we have heard it preached, "There is
none righteous, no, not one." This scripture is found in
Romans 3:10, but you must read the whole book. In the
first three chapters of Romans, the Apostle Paul by the
Holy Spirit is writing a serious indictment against man in
his natural state—that there is none righteous—which is
absolute truth!

But as we have previously discussed, Paul explains that our righteousness does not come through the Law or through our conduct. It comes only through faith in Jesus Christ and is "unto all and upon all them that believe..." (Romans 3:22).

We have read in Romans 5:17 that because of one man's offense—Adam's treason—death reigned in the world. Satan became the lord over mankind and everything man did was in response to fear—of death, of accident, of failure.

Do you know of anyone who has lived two or three hundred years because there wasn't enough death to go around? Of course not! There is an *abundance* of death in the world, but this scripture goes on to say, *"Much more* they which receive *abundance of grace* and of the *gift of righteousness* shall reign in life by one, Jesus Christ." Praise God!

Jesus bought the free gift of righteousness which was much more alive, much more real, and much more abundant than death. The fear of death is dispelled by life in Jesus Christ. As the Apostle Paul said, "O death, where is thy sting?" (1 Corinthians 15:55). The force of righteousness completely overcomes the power of sin and death like a bonfire overcomes a drop of water. We have more power over our lives as the righteousness of God in Jesus Christ than Satan had over us while we were in sin.

> *The fear of death is dispelled by life in Jesus Christ.*

Romans 5:17 in *The Amplified Bible* says, "...Much more surely will those who receive [God's] overflowing grace (unmerited favor) and the free gift of righteousness…*reign as kings in* life through the one Man Jesus Christ (the Messiah, the Anointed One)." When you make Jesus the Lord of your life, you receive the abundance of grace and the gift of righteousness to enable you to reign in life as a king! You will be in a position to reign over your life and the circumstances surrounding you the same as a king reigns over his kingdom.

The believer must learn to depend on his free gift of righteousness. He must learn to lean on it. This is one of the first things I found out from the Word of God. Satan told me I didn't have any right to be healed. He said I didn't have any right to receive the infilling of the Holy Spirit and that I certainly didn't have the right to minister to the needs of other people. Well, if I happened to feel a little sinful at the time, then I would agree with him.

Actually, I didn't realize Satan was telling me all those things. I thought they were my own ideas. Then I saw in the Word that I had a right to the gift of righteouness simply because Jesus gave me the right, and I saw that I had been made the righteousness of God, Himself.

Do you realize what "being made the righteousness of God" really means? You have to think about it in order to see the full reality there. The child, or heir, of a king has the same right as the king himself because he is part of the king. He is born of the king and, consequently, has the same legal rights and privileges. As the Apostle Paul wrote, even though the heir may be just a child and is still being tutored, he is nevertheless king of the land and has the authority to rule (Galatians 4:1-2).

When you were born again, the Bible says you became bone of His bone. You have rights and privileges because you have been born of the Spirit of God. God has been reproduced on the inside of you! These rights are yours because Jesus of Nazareth paid the price for the sin problem and caused you to be reborn.

Adam was born of God. If you'll read Genesis, you'll see that God created his body and then breathed into it the breath of life (Genesis 2:7). It was completely lifeless until God gave it life by breathing into it. Adam's life came from the inside of God, and essentially the same thing occurs in the new birth. You were dead in sins and trespasses until God re-created your spirit and gave you His life. When you accepted the sacrifice of Jesus, the Spirit of God hovered over your body and a new spirit life which had never existed before was birthed inside you.

When you discover who you are in Jesus, your entire existence—your health, your financial life, your social life—will take on new meaning. The storms of life will be stopped as you exert pressure on them with the Word of God and the power of the Holy Spirit dwelling within you. You are to reign as a king under your Lord and Savior, Jesus Christ of Nazareth! Hallelujah!

God sees you this way. He expects you to take your rightful place and live this kind of life, above the beggarly elements of the world. As a believer, He has given you the power and strength of the Holy Spirit as your Comforter and Jesus Christ as your Lord and High Priest, to change nations and governments around the world. Begin to take the New Testament seriously. Begin to believe it and walk in it and to lean hard on the righteousness which God has freely given you. You will then realize that all things are possible to you as a believer. You'll say, "Without Him I can do

> *God has given you the power and strength of the Holy Spirit and Jesus Christ as your Lord to change nations and governments around the world.*

nothing. But thank God, I have Him, and I can do all things through Christ which strengthens me" (Philippians 4:13). Your testimony will then be one of power and strength as your life is molded by the Holy Spirit.

As a born-again child of God, you are to be a superman in the eyes of the world, holding forth the Word of Life! When you cross the rough spots, you won't knuckle under—you'll stand tall and triumph over them. You'll walk hand in hand with Jesus through the storms of life and come out victoriously!

God doesn't put these storms and rough spots before you— He takes you through them and delivers you from them. Satan throws these things at you to stop you from acting on the Word and exercising your righteousness in Jesus Christ. Satan knows that these are dangerous spiritual weapons in the hands of a believer, so he is constantly trying to stop their effectiveness.

chapterseven
Become Righteousness-Minded

chapterseven

Become Righteousness-Minded

Paul said in 1 Corinthians 15:34, "Awake to righteousness, and sin not...." *Awake to righteousness.* Become aware that you have been made the righteousness of God in Jesus Christ, that you have been placed in right-standing with Him through the sacrifice of Jesus at Calvary. When you do, it will stop the sin in your life. As long as Satan can convince you that you don't have any right to the things of God, he can keep you under his thumb and sin will control your life. But when you awake to righteousness, you will realize that Satan is a defeated foe and the struggle is over.

Awake to righteousness...become righteousness-minded! You have been thoroughly equipped to handle every situation that comes your way. You are to reign in life as a king by Jesus Christ. You are to live in conformity with the Father. The Almighty God, Creator of the universe, chose to come down on your level in the form of Jesus Christ, to dwell in your heart by the Holy Spirit, and to give you His righteousness, His ability and His strength…"because greater is he that is in you, than he that is in the world" (1 John 4:4). Praise God!

Ephesians 3:20 says He is "…able to do exceeding abundantly above all that we ask or think, according to the power that worketh in us."

When I fully understood the significance of this scripture, I began to have some confidence in the ministry of the Holy Spirit in my life. In fact, the Lord spoke to my heart one day and said, *How much confidence are you placing in the God within you?* At that time, I had no confidence in Him whatsoever! I was praying and *hoping* God would do something—obviously, with no results. Then, I grasped the reality of the indwelling of the Holy Spirit of God.

Jesus said that when the Spirit of Truth came, He would reveal the things of God to us (John 16:13-15). God, through the Holy Spirit, began to reveal to my heart the deep truths of the new birth, of the righteousness of God in Jesus Christ. He revealed the power of the Holy Spirit—God's muscle, God's mind, God's everything—and He showed how this part of the Godhead was living inside every born-again, Spirit-filled believer! These truths became deeply rooted in my spirit, and I began to become righteousness-minded.

How do you become righteousness-minded? Romans 8:5 says, "For they that are after the flesh do mind the things of the flesh...." Hebrews 5:13 tells us, "For every one that useth milk is unskillful in the *word of righteousness:* for he is a babe." He doesn't know how to use the Bible—how to believe it or how to fight Satan with it. Verse 14 says, "But strong meat belongeth to them that are of full age, even those who by reason of use have their senses exercised to discern both good and evil."

Proverbs 4:20 instructs us to attend to the Word of God. In the past we have not done this. We have occupied ourselves much of the time with fleshly things. We have thought *sickness* instead of healing...*weakness* instead of strength...*trouble* instead of victory...*poverty* instead of prosperity...*sin* instead of righteousness. We have attended to these other things, almost completely ignoring the power of the Word of God to deliver us from the flesh.

Only by feeding on the Word will we grow and be able to overcome the things of the flesh and function in line with God. I can speak from experience because I was overweight and hooked on cigarettes. For several years, I fought against my body with little success; but when I grew in the Word of God and began to walk in the spirit, I no longer fulfilled the lusts of the flesh. When I learned that I could control my physical body, my weight came down to normal and the smoking habit was broken!

chaptereight

Success in
Righteousness

Success in Righteousness

A person who thinks "righteousness" instead of "sin" is valuable to God, to himself, and to the people around him. He will always be there when you need him. This is not true of the sin-minded, defeat-minded Christian. There is a very deceitful area here that most people have fallen into at some time in their lives, without realizing it. I have heard the following many times and have been guilty of saying it myself: "Well, we're praying about this situation, and if the doors are open, then it's God's will for us to go; but if they're not, then it must not be God's will."

Folks, if the "open door" is evidence of the will of God, then the Apostle Paul was never in God's will! He encountered obstacles and barriers throughout his entire ministry, but he took the Word of God and knocked the doors open in order to get the job done! Even when he was thrown in prison, he prayed his way out. He did his job, despite the obstacles.

Sin consciousness will look for a way *out* of a situation: "We might not have enough money to go" or "I might not be able to take off work." However, a righteousness consciousness always finds a way in. When I was preaching in Jamaica, there was a man who had quit a good job in order to attend our

> *A righteousness consciousness always finds a way in.*

meetings and hear the Word. He would walk six miles twice each day just to be in the meetings, and when I questioned him about it, he said, "Brother Copeland, I fasted and prayed for a year that God would send someone to teach us the Word, and I'm not going to miss out on any of it! With what I'm learning about faith from the Word, I can get a better job!"

You see, this man was looking for a way in! He wanted more of the things of God. He knew that Jesus had said, "But seek ye first the kingdom of God, and his righteousness; and all these things shall be added unto you" (Matthew 6:33).

Another area where many people have been deceived is in "putting out a fleece." The person who uses a fleece is depending on a physical sign of God's will in a situation, and if he's not watchful, he'll get fleeced!

Now, Gideon used a fleece, but let's analyze his situation for a moment. In the first place, Gideon was not a reborn man. Consequently, he was forced to rely on physical evidence. He had no knowledge of God whatsoever because his entire family was following Baal. Second, there was no prophet in the land to give him the Word of God, and the prophet was the only source of revelation knowledge in those days. Third, Gideon was dealing with an angel—something completely foreign to him. Therefore, in his position, he had no choice but to put out a fleece, to get a physical sign, showing him what to do.

As believers, you and I are not in Gideon's position. We have been born again and are led by the Spirit of God. We have access to the Holy Spirit, and have the written Word of God to use as a guide in finding God's will for our lives. If you don't know what to do in a particular situation, go to the Word of God, spend some time in prayer, meditate in the Word, and the Lord will begin to lead you. He said, "My sheep hear my voice..." (John 10:27).

You will know what to do by the leadership of the Holy Spirit. We don't have to depend on a sign from the natural, physical world to lead us. We are not blind. We have spiritual eyes, and we are to use them. Also, when you put out a fleece in the natural world, you are giving Satan a chance to foul up the situation, since the physical world is his field of operation.

Here is a three-step formula which, when used seriously, will cause success in every area of your life. Nothing can stop it. Every Christian endeavor, no matter what it is, will succeed when backed with this kind of prayer and dedication because God is behind it.

1. *Find the will of God in your situation by prayer and meditation in the Word.*

2. *Once you have found the will of God, confer no longer with flesh and blood.* Don't ask other people what to do. I may discuss a situation with my wife or my staff, but once we have prayed and I know the will of God, then it doesn't matter what they think or say about it.

3. *Get your job done at all costs.* Don't allow anything or anyone to stand in the way of God's will.

In order for a believer to live this kind of successful life, he must come to the realization that he has complete access to the ministry of Jesus. Jesus said in John 16:13-15, "Howbeit when he, the Spirit of truth, is come...he shall receive of mine, and shall show it unto you. All things that the Father hath are mine: therefore said I, that he shall take of mine, and shall show it unto you." What a statement! This is almost more than the human mind can comprehend.

> *As a new creation in Christ, you have the Name of Jesus, the Word of God, and the Spirit of God to enable you to stand and minister in the place of Jesus.*

The Spirit of God has been sent into an earthly ministry just as legal and real as Jesus' earthly ministry. Jesus came to provide the way for us, and the Holy Spirit has come to teach us the way. Jesus came to fulfill the Abrahamic covenant. The Holy Spirit has come to see that the Christian covenant is fulfilled.

The Spirit of God did not take the place of Jesus—He is God the Holy Spirit, and He is fulfilling His own ministry as God the

Father directed Him.

The Word of God and the Name of Jesus have taken Jesus' place here on earth. He said, "As long as I am in the world, I am the light of the world" (John 9:5), and "...believe in the light, that ye may be the children of light" (John 12:36). As a new creation in Christ, you have the Name of Jesus, the Word of God, and the Spirit of God to enable you to stand and minister in the place of Jesus.

chapternine

Benefits of Righteousness

chapternine

Benefits of Righteousness

As a believer, you have total access to the ministry of Jesus, the ministry of the Holy Spirit and all that the Father has. To receive from Him, all you have to do is go to His Word! The only reason we have been such easy targets for Satan is because we have not known our rights and privileges in Jesus Christ. Therefore, he could easily usurp authority over us. But the Bible says we have authority to tread on serpents and scorpions and over all the power of the enemy (Luke 10:19).

We must find out what the Word has to say about the things of life and then walk in line with it. We must renew our minds and put the force of righteousness to work in our lives.

If you are led by what you see or how you feel, you will fail. When you lean on your righteousness in Jesus Christ, you know what belongs to you and you won't lie down under sickness or any other attack of Satan. You will go to the Word concerning healing, receive it for yourself, and walk in faith on it because it is the Word of your Father.

Almighty God is your very own Father! You are bone of His bone, spirit of His Spirit, a joint heir with Jesus Christ, and living in the kingdom of God. As you realize these things in your life, you become God-inside-minded. You no longer think of God as being a million miles away. He is residing inside you!

Righteousness then, becomes a force in the life of a believer which undergirds his faith. The reality of righteousness enables a believer to do the impossible. Jesus approached the tomb of Lazarus and said, "Take ye away the stone..." (John 11:39). He never wavered in His faith.

> *Righteousness becomes a force in the life of a believer which undergirds his faith.*

Actually, throughout His ministry, Jesus showed neither a lack of faith nor an abundance of faith. He simply knew who He was and took advantage of the authority that was His. You might say, "Yes, of course, He did—He was the Son of God!" Well, who are you? John 1:12 says, "But as many as received him, to them gave he power to become the sons of God, even to them that believe on his name." Romans 8:14 says, "For as many as are led by the Spirit of God, they are the sons of God."

I have heard it argued that we will not receive our rights as sons of God until we get to heaven. However, Philippians 2:15-

16 says, "That ye may be blameless and harmless, the sons of God, without rebuke, in the midst of a crooked and perverse nation, among whom ye shine as lights in the world; holding forth the word of life...."

There is no crooked and perverse generation in heaven. The only crooked and perverse generation is here on earth and this is where we are to be the sons of God and hold forth the Word.

We are told, "Let this mind be in you, which was also in Christ Jesus" (Philippians 2:5). Jesus never stopped to think whether He had enough faith. He merely acted according to His rights in the kingdom of God. He stepped to the mouth of Lazarus' tomb with a divine assurance, illustrating His conscious right-standing with God—His righteousness consciousness. Jesus revealed what righteousness really is.

Is it reasonable? No. Is it real? Yes, regardless of what the natural mind says, and it will work in the life of a Christian.

Look at the apostles after the day of Pentecost. They had a right-standing relationship with God, and it was working in their lives. Peter stood and preached the Word, ministering boldly in the Name of Jesus. After all

The righteousness of God in Jesus Christ is the driving force behind our faith, causing us to triumph in His Name.

his failures, he realized that God loved him and that his past had been wiped away. He was filled with the Spirit of God and was doing the things Joel had prophesied would be done.

The righteousness of God in Jesus Christ is the driving

force behind our faith, causing us to triumph in His Name.

Jesus triumphed over Satan in three areas. First, during His earthly ministry, He spoke to Satan and said, "It is written…" (Matthew 4:4, 7, 10), and Satan had to obey the Word of God. Secondly, at the cross and resurrection, Jesus stripped Satan of his power and took the keys of hell and death.

However, the third and most important area of Jesus' triumph over Satan is His victory in the new birth. It was impossible in Satan's thinking for God to take a man in sin, turn him into righteousness, give him the armor of God and enable him to triumph as Jesus did. This is victory of the highest order! Sin turned into *righteousness!* Death turned into *life!*

chapterten

The Triumph of
Righteousness

chapterten

The Triumph of Righteousness

Righteousness triumphs in the face of Satan and the whole world. No devil in hell is big enough to stop it, and it is available to "whosoever will." All are the same in the eyes of God. All need the power of God.

When we cry out to God in the Name of Jesus, He receives us with open arms, virtually re-creating us. He then gives us His righteousness, and makes us powerhouses of faith! It is happening today all over the world to people in every walk of life!

God sees the believer as *righteousness.* In 2 Corinthians 6:14 Paul wrote, "Be ye not unequally yoked together with unbelievers: for what fellowship hath righteousness with unrighteousness? and what communion hath light with darkness?" Here, the Word refers to the believer as righteousness and light and the unbelievers as unrighteousness and darkness.

We are the light of the world. Praise God!

We, as believers, have His righteousness. We are the crowning creation of God! A reborn man is the greatest creation in the universe! Man in his natural, sinful state was headed straight to hell. By all laws, he deserved to be condemned forever, but God intervened and legally changed the laws. He beat Satan at his own game, and life became ruler over death! Jesus became the Lord and Champion of our salvation. He became the Bishop over our souls in the new birth. He gave us His righteousness—the ability to triumph in His Name—and we have peace with God.

He, who knew no sin, was made to be sin. He was made to be our sinfulness so that we could be made His righteousness.

We have been made to sit with Him in heavenly places in Christ Jesus—victorious in Him.

We have been made to sit with Him in heavenly places in Christ Jesus—victorious in Him. This is real victory!

We don't just bow a subservient knee to God—we join our faith with His, giving Him the opportunity to do a miracle in our hearts and turn us into the righteousness of Almighty God!

Now we can approach the throne of grace boldly—without a sense of fear or condemnation—and receive from our Father all that is ours as a new creation in Christ.

Prayer for Salvation and Baptism in the Holy Spirit

Heavenly Father, I come to You in the Name of Jesus. Your Word says, "Whosoever shall call on the name of the Lord shall be saved" (Acts 2:21). I am calling on You. I pray and ask Jesus to come into my heart and be Lord over my life according to Romans 10:9-10: "If thou shalt confess with thy mouth the Lord Jesus, and shalt believe in thine heart that God hath raised him from the dead, thou shalt be saved. For with the heart man believeth unto righteousness; and with the mouth confession is made unto salvation." I do that now. I confess that Jesus is Lord, and I believe in my heart that God raised Him from the dead.

I am now reborn! I am a Christian—a child of Almighty God! I am saved! You also said in Your Word, "If ye then, being evil, know how to give good gifts unto your children: HOW MUCH MORE shall your heavenly Father give the Holy Spirit to them that ask him?" (Luke 11:13). I'm also asking You to fill me with the Holy Spirit. Holy Spirit, rise up within me as I praise God. I fully expect to speak with other tongues as You give me the utterance (Acts 2:4). In Jesus' Name. Amen!

Begin to praise God for filling you with the Holy Spirit. Speak those words and syllables you receive—not in your own language, but the language given to you by the Holy Spirit. You have to use your own voice. God will not force you to speak. Don't be concerned with how it sounds. It is a heavenly language!

Continue with the blessing God has given you and pray in the spirit every day.

You are a born-again, Spirit-filled believer. You'll never be the same!

Find a good church that boldly preaches God's Word and obeys it. Become part of a church family who will love and care for you as you love and care for them.

We need to be connected to each other. It increases our strength in God. It's God's plan for us.

Make it a habit to watch the *Believer's Voice of Victory* television broadcast and become a doer of the Word, who is blessed in his doing (James 1:22-25).

About the Author

Kenneth Copeland is co-founder and president of Kenneth Copeland Ministries in Fort Worth, Texas, and best-selling author of books that include *How to Discipline Your Flesh* and *Honor—Walking in Honesty, Truth and Integrity*.

Now in his 43rd year as a minister of the gospel of Christ and teacher of God's Word, Kenneth is the recording artist of such award-winning albums as his Grammy-nominated *Only the Redeemed, In His Presence, He Is Jehovah, Just a Closer Walk* and his most recently released *Big Band Gospel* album. He also co-stars as the character Wichita Slim in the children's adventure videos *The Gunslinger, Covenant Rider* and the movie *The Treasure of Eagle Mountain,* and as Daniel Lyon in the *Commander Kellie and the Superkids*_{TM} videos *Armor of Light* and *Judgment: The Trial of Commander Kellie.*

With the help of offices and staff in the United States, Canada, England, Australia, South Africa and Ukraine, Kenneth is fulfilling his vision to boldly preach the uncompromised Word of God from the top of this world, to the bottom, and all the way around. His ministry reaches millions of people worldwide through daily and Sunday TV broadcasts, magazines, teaching audios and videos, conventions and campaigns, and the World Wide Web.

World Offices
Kenneth Copeland Ministries

For more information about KCM and our products,
please write to the office nearest you:

Kenneth Copeland Ministries
Fort Worth, TX 76192-0001

Kenneth Copeland
Locked Bag 2600
Mansfield Delivery Centre
QUEENSLAND 4122
AUSTRALIA

Kenneth Copeland
Post Office Box 15
BATH
BA1 3XN
U.K.

Kenneth Copeland
Private Bag X 909
FONTAINEBLEAU
2032
REPUBLIC OF
SOUTH AFRICA

Kenneth Copeland
PO Box 3111 STN LCD 1
Langley BC V3A 4R3
CANADA

Kenneth Copeland Ministries
Post Office Box 84
L'VIV 79000
UKRAINE

We're Here for You!

Join Kenneth and Gloria Copeland and the *Believer's Voice of Victory* broadcasts Monday through Friday and on Sunday each week, and learn how faith in God's Word can take your life from ordinary to extraordinary.

You can catch the *Believer's Voice of Victory* broadcast on your local, cable or satellite channels.* And it's also available 24 hours a day by webcast at BVOV.TV.

Enjoy inspired teaching and encouragement from Kenneth and Gloria Copeland and guest ministers each month in the *Believer's Voice of Victory* magazine. Also included are real-life testimonies of God's miraculous power and divine intervention in the lives of people just like you!

To receive a FREE subscription to
Believer's Voice of Victory, write to:
Kenneth Copeland Ministries
Fort Worth, TX 76192-0001
Or call: 800-600-7395
Or visit: **www.kcm.org**

If you are writing from outside the U.S., please contact the KCM office nearest you. Addresses for all Kenneth Copeland Ministries offices are listed on the previous page.

* Check your local listings for times and stations in your area.